OTHER HELEN EXLEY GIFTBOOKS:
Thoughts on Being at Peace
Thoughts on Being Happy
Wishing you Happiness
With Deepest Sympathy

EDITED BY HELEN EXLEY
BORDER ILLUSTRATIONS BY SHARON BASSIN

Published simultaneously in 1996 by Exley Publications
in Great Britain, and Exley Giftbooks in the USA.

12 11 10 9 8 7 6 5 4 3

Picture and text selection by © Helen Exley 1996.
Border Illustrations © Sharon Bassin 1996.

ISBN 1-85015-712-X

Designed by Pinpoint Design.
Picture research by P. A. Goldberg and J. Clift/Image Select.
Typeset by Delta, Watford.
Printed and bound in China.

Exley Publications Ltd, 16 Chalk Hill, Watford,
Herts WD1 4BN, UK.
Exley Giftbooks, 232 Madison Avenue, Suite 1206,
NY 10016, USA.

Words of COMFORT

A Helen Exley Giftbook

EXLEY
NEW YORK • WATFORD, UK

THE NEXT ROOM

Death is nothing at all... I have only slipped away into the next room. I am I, and you are you. Whatever we were to each other, that we still are. Call me by my old familiar name, speak to me in the easy way which you always used. Put no difference in your tone, wear no forced air of solemnity or sorrow. Laugh as we always laughed at the little jokes we enjoyed together. Pray, smile, think of me – let my name be ever the household word that it always was, let it be spoken without effect, without the trace of a shadow on it. Life means all that it ever meant. It is the same as it ever was, there is unbroken continuity. Why should I be out of mind because I am out of sight? I am waiting for you, for an interval, somewhere very near, just round the corner. All is well.

CANON HENRY SCOTT HOLLAND

I wish this poem
was an arm around you
which could
comfort you.

I wish this poem
was a room,
with a glowing fire in it
so that you could
curl yourself up.

I wish that this
was so much more
for you.

I wish you could
wish on this poem.

And then, maybe,
you wouldn't cry.

HENRYK BOROWSKI, AGED 17

THE EXISTENCE OF LOVE

I had thought that your death
Was a waste and a destruction,
A pain of grief hardly to be endured.
I am only beginning to learn
That your life was a gift and a growing
And a loving left with me.
The desperation of death
Destroyed the existence of love,
But the fact of death
Cannot destroy what has been given.
I am learning to look at your life again
Instead of your death and your departing.

Marjorie Pizer

I AM THE GENTLE
AUTUMN'S RAIN

Do not stand at my grave and weep;
I am not there.
I do not sleep.
I am a thousand winds that blow.
I am the diamond glints on snow.
I am the sunlight on ripened grain.
I am the gentle autumn's rain.
When you awaken in the morning's hush,
I am the swift uplifting rush
Of quiet birds in circled flight.
I am the soft stars that shine at night.
Do not stand at my grave and cry;
I am not there.
I did not die.

ANONYMOUS

MUSIC I HEARD WITH YOU

Music I heard with you was more than music,
And bread I broke with you was more than bread;
Now that I am without you, all is desolate;
All that was once so beautiful is dead.

Your hands once touched this table and this silver,
And I have seen your fingers hold this glass.
These things do not remember you, beloved, –
And yet your touch upon them will not pass.

For it was in my heart you moved among them,
And blessed them with your hands and with
    your eyes;
And in my heart they will remember always, –
They knew you once, O beautiful and wise.

CONRAD AIKEN

SEASONS OF LIFE

Out of every crisis comes the chance to be reborn, to reconceive ourselves as individuals, to choose the kind of change that will help us to grow and to fulfil ourselves more completely.

NENA O'NEILL

Your pain is the breaking of the shell that encloses your understanding. Even as the stone of the fruit must break, that its heart may stand in the sun, so must you know pain.

KAHLIL GIBRAN, FROM "THE PROPHET"

But to see the Spring, really to see it, you must have lived through the Winter first.

RUMER GODDEN, FROM "KINGFISHERS CATCH FIRE"

The real value of ease cannot be appreciated without having known pain, nor of sweetness without having tasted bitterness, nor of good without having seen evil, nor even of life itself without having passed through death.

SADHU SUNDAR SINGH

STRENGTH BORN OF PAIN

I would say to those who mourn... look upon each day that comes as a challenge, as a test of courage. The pain will come in waves, some days worse than others, for no apparent reason. Accept the pain. Do not suppress it. Never attempt to hide grief from yourself. Little by little, just as the deaf, the blind, the handicapped develop with time an extra sense to balance disability, so the bereaved, the widowed, will find new strength, new vision, born of the very pain and loneliness which seem, at first, impossible to master.

DAPHNE DU MAURIER,
FROM "THE REBECCA NOTEBOOK"

Your happiness has been ripped apart. The mind is in shock. There seems no hope, no joy, no purpose in living.

But you are of a species bred to endure. The sufferings of others do not make your own less real – but remember how those others clung to life and, in the end, won through.

You can do it.

The old happiness is withered and dead. But, see, there is a greenness veiling the land... the frail beginnings of a new and better life.

PAM BROWN

A new life begins for us with every second. Let us go forward joyously to meet it. We must press on, whether we will or no, and we shall walk better with our eyes before us than with them ever cast behind.

JEROME K. JEROME

JUST TO BE ALIVE

I like living.
I have sometimes been
wildly, despairingly,
acutely miserable,
racked with sorrow,
but through it all I still know
quite certainly that just to be alive
is a grand thing.

AGATHA CHRISTIE

There is kindness in the world – and wisdom and courtesy and love. In city tenements, in deserts, forests, villages – in this town. This street. Never forget.

PAM BROWN

Life is not made up of great sacrifices and duties, but of little things; in which smiles and kindness given habitually are what win and preserve the heart and secure comfort.

SIR HUMPHRY DAVY

Sometimes our light goes out but it is blown again into flame by an encounter with another human being. Each of us owes the deepest thanks to those who have rekindled this inner light.

ALBERT SCHWEITZER

GOING THROUGH THE GRIEF

Grief discriminates against no one. It kills. Maims. And cripples. It is the ashes from which the phoenix rises, and the mettle of re-birth. It returns life to the living dead. It teaches that there is nothing absolutely true, or untrue. It assures the living that we know nothing for certain. It humbles. It shrouds. It blackens. It enlightens.

Grief will make a new person out of you, if it doesn't kill you in the making.

STEPHANIE ERICSSON

To shirk pain, bearable pain, altogether is not only to be less real than one might have been: it is to isolate oneself from the common lot of pain, from the pain of humanity and the world. It is to blunt or cut off or withdraw one's antennae; it is to play only such notes as one chooses in the universal symphony, which is a symphony of suffering as well as of joy.

VICTOR GOLLANCZ

LOVE IS NEVER LOST

As the months pass and the seasons change,
something of tranquillity descends, and
although the well-remembered footstep will not
sound again, nor the voice call from the room
beyond, there seems to be about one in the air
an atmosphere of love, a living presence.

DAPHNE DU MAURIER, FROM "THE REBECCA NOTEBOOK"

And when one of us is gone
And one is left alone to carry on
Well then remembering will have to do
Our memories alone will get us through
Think about the days of me and you
Of you and me against the world.

PAUL WILLIAMS AND KEN ASCHER

Nothing rooted in love is ever lost, for it has
become part of the living whole.

PAM BROWN

Though they sink through the sea they shall
   rise again;
Though lovers be lost love shall not;
And death shall have no dominion.

DYLAN THOMAS

The life that I have
Is all that I have
And the life that I have
Is yours
The love that I have
Of the life that I have
Is yours, and yours, and yours.
A sleep I shall have
A rest I shall have
Yet death will be but a pause,
For the peace of my years
In the long green grass
Will be yours, and yours, and yours.

LEO-MARKS

The true way of softening one's troubles is to solace those of others.

MADAME DE MAINTENON

Let us make one point... that we meet each other with a smile, when it is difficult to smile... smile at each other, make time for each other.

MOTHER TERESA

It is one of the most beautiful compensations of this life that no man can sincerely try to help another without helping himself.

RALPH WALDO EMERSON

Do not grieve. Misfortunes will happen to the wisest and best of men. Death will come, always out of season. It is the command of the Great Spirit, and all nations and people must obey. What is past and what cannot be prevented should not be grieved for…. Misfortunes do not flourish particularly in our lives – they grow everywhere.

Big Elk, Omaha Chief

And you would accept the seasons of your heart, even as you have always accepted the seasons that pass over your fields. And you would watch with serenity through the winters of your grief.

Kahlil Gibran, from "The Prophet"

This existence of ours is as transient as autumn clouds.
To watch the birth and death of beings is like looking at the movements of a dance.
A lifetime is a flash of lightning in the sky.
Rushing by, like a torrent down a steep mountain.

Buddha

I SHALL ALWAYS BE NEAR YOU

If I do not return, my dear Sarah, never forget how much I loved you, nor that when my last breath escapes me on the battlefield, it will whisper your name.... "If the dead can come back to this earth and flit unseen around those they loved, I shall always be near you; in the gladdest days and in the darkest nights... *always* always, and if there be a soft breeze upon your cheek, it shall be my breath, as the cool air fans your throbbing temple, it shall be my spirit...."

MAJOR SULLIVAN BALLOU,
FROM A LETTER TO HIS WIFE, SARAH, JUST ONE WEEK BEFORE THE
FIRST BATTLE OF BULL RUN, IN WHICH MAJOR BALLOU WAS KILLED

I don't think then of all the misery, but of the beauty that still remains. This is one of the things that Mummy and I are so entirely different about. Her counsel when one feels melancholy is "Think of all the misery in the world and be thankful that you are not sharing in it!" My advice is: "Go outside, to the fields, enjoy nature and the sunshine, go out and try to recapture happiness in yourself and in God. Think of all the beauty that's still left in and around you and be happy!"

ANNE FRANK

Some of the greatest achievements of humankind have come from people suffering under great burdens – loss and imprisonment, sickness and deprivation. They demonstrate as no others can the dignity and power of the human spirit. Beethoven wrote his most noble and imaginative works after deafness had overtaken him. Milton wrote from blindness. Bunyan from jail. Stephen Hawking surveys the universe from a wheelchair. The persecuted raise their voices from oppression to speak for their people. The disfigured in war bring hope to the deprived.

Some are only known to a few. Some are never recognized. But they tell us not to be afraid. There is work still to be done. There are things to be achieved. There is beauty to be created. There are puzzles to be solved. There is happiness to be had.

The world is full of marvels. Accept them and be glad. Do not let anything deprive you of a love for life.

PAM BROWN

... THROUGH THE RAIN

O joy, that seekest me through pain,
I cannot close my heart to thee;
I trace the rainbow through the rain,
And feel the promise is not vain
That morn shall tearless be.

GEORGE MATHESON

Nothing can help us face the unknown future
with more courage and optimism than
remembering the glory moments, and everybody
has a few of them.

Eda LeShan

If you keep a green bough in your heart,
the singing bird will come.

Chinese Proverb

Walk on a rainbow trail; walk on a trail of song,
and all about you will be beauty. There is a way
out of every dark mist, over a rainbow trail.

Navajo Song

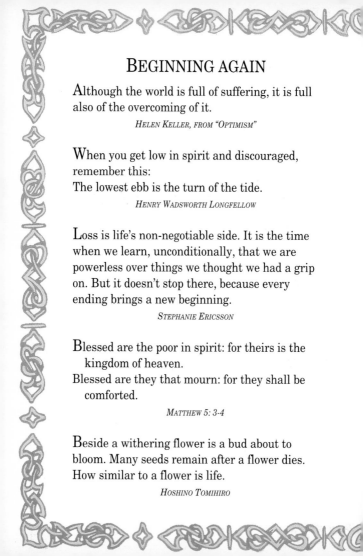

BEGINNING AGAIN

Although the world is full of suffering, it is full also of the overcoming of it.

HELEN KELLER, FROM "OPTIMISM"

When you get low in spirit and discouraged, remember this:
The lowest ebb is the turn of the tide.

HENRY WADSWORTH LONGFELLOW

Loss is life's non-negotiable side. It is the time when we learn, unconditionally, that we are powerless over things we thought we had a grip on. But it doesn't stop there, because every ending brings a new beginning.

STEPHANIE ERICSSON

Blessed are the poor in spirit: for theirs is the
    kingdom of heaven.
Blessed are they that mourn: for they shall be
    comforted.

MATTHEW 5: 3-4

Beside a withering flower is a bud about to bloom. Many seeds remain after a flower dies. How similar to a flower is life.

HOSHINO TOMIHIRO

I was taught these words by my grandmother as a phrase that is to be used at *all* times in your life. When things are spectacularly dreadful; when things are absolutely appalling; when everything is superb and wonderful and marvellous and happy – say these four words to yourself. They will give you a sense of perspective and help you also to make the most of what is good and be stoical about what is bad.

THIS TOO WILL PASS

CLAIRE RAYNER

The only courage that matters is the kind that gets you from one moment to the next.

MIGNON MCLAUGHLIN

Have courage for the great sorrows of life and patience for the small ones. And when you have finished your daily task, go to sleep in peace.

VICTOR HUGO

If the future seems overwhelming, remember that it comes one moment at a time.

BETH MENDE CONNY

BEAUTY AND SORROW

When we return from... happiness to self-awareness and to our knowledge of life's misery, our joy returns to sadness, the world shows us not its radiant sky but the blackness underneath, and then beauty and art make us sad. But they remain beautiful, they remain divine, and this is true of the fugue, the painting, the gull's tail feathers, the oil spot, and of far lesser things.

And even though the joy of forgetting oneself and the world lasts only for brief moments, the sorrow-steeped enchantment that rises from the miracle of beauty can endure for hours, for a lifetime.

HERMANN HESSE

WE WILL REMEMBER

They shall grow not old, as we that are left
  grow old:
Age shall not weary them nor the years condemn.
At the going down of the sun, and in the
  morning,
We will remember them.

LAURENCE BINYON, FROM "FOR THE FALLEN (SEPTEMBER 1914)"

WE CANNOT SEE

'Twill all be well: no need of care;
Though how it will,
   and when or where,
We cannot see, and can't declare.
In spite of dreams, in spite of thought,
'Tis not in vain and not for nought
The wind it blows, the ship it goes,
Though where and whither
   no one knows.

ARTHUR HUGH CLOUGH

All is but grief, and heavily we call
On the last terror for the end of all.
Then comes the happy moment: not a stir
In any tree, no portent in the sky:
The morn doth neither hasten nor defer,
The morrow hath no name to call it by,
But life and joy are one – we know not why, –
As though our very blood long breathless lain
Had tasted of the breath of God again.

ROBERT BRIDGES

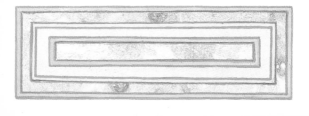

Those who have suffered most greatly often speak, with reticence, of the moment when pain and deprivation ceased to dominate, and quietness came – whenever the persecutors lost their power and became objects of pity. All human beings hold that living silence, that well of peace, at the core of their being.

PAM BROWN

There is nothing to save, now all is lost, but a tiny core of stillness in the heart like the eye of a violet.

D.H. LAWRENCE

THE TRIUMPH OF LIFE

I am emerging from an ocean of grief,
From the sorrow of many deaths,
From the inevitability of tragedy,
From the losing of love,
From the terrible triumph of destruction.
I am seeing the living that is to be lived,
The laughter that is to be laughed,
The joy that is to be enjoyed,
The loving that is to be accomplished.
I am learning at last
The tremendous triumph of life.

MARJORIE PIZER

Weeping may endure for a night, but the
morning brings a shout of joy.

PSALM 30:5

Acknowledgements: The publishers are grateful for permission to reproduce copyright material. While every effort has been made to trace copyright holders, the publishers would be pleased to hear from any not here acknowledged. ROBERT BRIDGES: Reprinted by permission of Lord Bridges. LAURENCE BINYON: Extract from "For The Fallen (September 1914)" by permission of Mrs Nicolete Gray, and The Society of Authors on behalf of the Laurence Binyon Estate. C.S. LEWIS: Extract from "A Grief Observed" published in *"A Book of Consolations"* by Faber & Faber. Reprinted by permission of HarperCollins Publishers Ltd. C.S. Lewis Pte. Ltd. 1960. PAUL WILLIAMS AND KEN ASCHER: Extract from "You and Me Against the World" published in *"Marriage"* Paul Williams Songbook. © 1974 Almo Music Corp. (ASCAP) All rights administered by Almo Music Corp. (ASCAP) for the world. All rights reserved International © secured. Used by permission. CONRAD AIKEN: "Discordants, Part I", from *Collected Poems,* 2nd edition © 1953, 1970 by Conrad Aiken, reprinted by permission of Oxford University Press, N.Y. MARJORIE PIZER: Extracts from "To You the Living" and "The Existence of Love" reprinted by permission of Second Back Row Press. DAPHNE DU MAURIER: Extracts from *"The Rebecca Notebook"* reprinted by permission of Curtis Brown on behalf of the Estate of Daphne du Maurier. KAHLIL GIBRAN: Extract from *"The Prophet"* by Kahlil Gibran reprinted by permission of Alfred A. Knopf Inc. 1923 by Kahlil Gibran and renewed 1951 by Administrators C.T.A. of Kahlil Gibran Estate and Mary G. Gibran. D. H. LAWRENCE: Extract from "Nothing To Save" reprinted by permission of Laurence Pollinger Ltd. on behalf of the Estate of D. H. Lawrence. DYLAN THOMAS: Extract from "And Death Shall Have No Dominion", from the Poems of Dylan Thomas. Copyright © 1945 by the Trustees for the Copyrights of Dylan Thomas. Reprinted by permission of David Higham Associates Ltd. and New Directions Publishing Corporation. NORAH LENEY: "Grief" published in *"Love And Lost"* ed. Frances Lindsay-Hills, Chosen Heritage Ltd., 1994. From *"In A Lifetime"* published by JMR Publishing N.Y. 1975.

Picture Credits: Exley Publications would like to thank the following organizations and individuals for permission to reproduce their pictures: Art Resource (AR), The Bridgeman Art Library (BAL), Edimedia (EDI), Fine Art Photographic (FAP), Scala (SCA). Cover: Herbert Gustave Schmalz, Yellow Roses, BAL; title page: © 1996 Dorothea Sharp, Flowerpiece, BAL; p6: © 1996 Patrick William Adam, BAL; p8: Princess Antonia of Portugal, EDI; p11: © 1996 Blanche Camus, The Open Window, Christie's; p12: © 1996 Karen Armitage, Arrangement in a glass vase, BAL; p14: © 1996 Diana Armfield, Anemones, BAL; p16: Walter Crane, Madonna Lilies, BAL; p19: George Seurat, BAL; p20: © 1996 Karen Armitage, Chrysanthemum, Snowcap, BAL; p22: Albert Ernest Brockbank, FAP; p24: Nikolai Astrup, By the Open Door, Sotheby's; p27: John Atkinson Grimshaw, A Moonlit Lane, BAL; p29: © 1996 Claude Monet, The Luncheon, AR; p31: © 1996 Vernon Ward, Daffodils, 1965, BAL; 32: Blanche Hoschedé; p34: © 1996 Nesta Jennings Campbell, Shades of Night, BAL; p37: Isaac Snowman, A Letter of Love, BAL; p38: © 1996 Kevin Macpherson, Rose Garden, Image Bank; p40: Ernest Spence, The Garden, FAP; p42: © 1996 Peter Kettle; p45: © 1996 Henri Martin, A Garden in the Sunshine, BAL; p47: © 1996 Peter Vilhelm Ilsted, A Girl Reading by a Window, Sotheby's; p49: John Atkinson Grimshaw, The Timber Waggon, BAL; p51: © 1996 Bruno Guaitamacchi, Mountain Flowers, BAL; p52: © 1996 Hugh L. Norris, Burton Bradstock, Dorset, BAL; p54: © 1996 Aleksandr Gherasimov, SCA; p57: Emile Claus, SCA; p58: Lucien Frank, FAP; p61: © 1996 Ellen Fradgley, A Rose Arbour and Old Well, Venice, BAL.